HOW TO WRITE A PLAY

Journal AND Workbook

CREATED BY TRISHA SUGAREK

~~ Much more than a journal for your creative writing,
this workbook provides
the playwright with the 'how to's' of writing a play. ~~

But I LOVE this paragraph. How can I delete it? It's some of my best writing ever! Ok, maybe it doesn't contribute to the overall story but I spent so long writing it! If single paragraphs could win the Pulitzer, th[...]aph would win, for sur[...]evision is overrated, [...] since I spent so much time [...] this par[...]graph. Why [...] to get rid of something th[...] [...]u can't make [...] [...] This parag[...] [...] I

This journal belongs to:

_____

Notice

Made in the USA   ISBN: 9781087232508

Ink drawings by Trisha Sugarek
Cover and Interior Design by David White

To view all of the author's fiction and play scripts go to:
www.writeratplay.com

Table of Contents

"What would you write if you weren't afraid?"

- Mary Y-Arr

Introduction

I created this journal/workbook to encourage other playwrights to pursue their dreams. It doesn't matter that you are just beginning your journey as a writer. Whatever your level of writing may be I have tried to create a journal for the playwright inside all of us. Perhaps you have been journaling for years and want to try your hand at a stage script. Or you are a more experienced writer and need a little inspiration to get you started on your next project. Regardless of your experience, I hope you find this journal encouraging and a safe place to store your characters, your story outlines, and your private ideas for future plays.

Only when I began to write seriously did I come to realize that I had been writing my entire adult life. But back then I considered it just 'scribbling'.

A thought I didn't want to forget, or a feeling I had to capture. Or a phrase that I was inspired by.

I have written over fifty plays of all lengths. 30 of these are short, often ten minute, plays for teens in the classroom. No sets, no props, no costumes. Being an actor and then a director (in a past life) I have read hundreds of scripts and I urge you to do the same. It's great research on being a better playwright.

But most important, have fun. Stop to enjoy the process. You will stumble and fall. If you write something that is bad, remember, that's what re-writes are for!

"The difference between the right word and the nearly right word is the same as that between lightning and the lightning bug."

Mark Twain

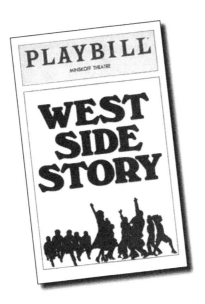

How to Begin

To stare at a blank page or screen this is the scariest thing of all and sometimes causes a writer to give up before they have begun. Ray Bradbury said, "*Writing is supposed to be difficult, agonizing, a dreadful exercise, a terrible occupation.*"

Forget for a moment about writing a Tony award winning stage play. Begin with the first outline of your story. Don't let people tell you it starts with the first word that's just silly. Practice writing that *first* piece of dialogue. For example:

SAM. (*Pulling the stranger out of the street.*) Watch out! Didn't you see that bus bearing down on you?

JANE. (*Clinging to his arm.*) No. I wasn't thinking I didn't see thank you.

And…

BILL. (*Sitting at the steel table.*) What the hell am I doing here? What was I thinking visiting a convicted killer?'

And…

VIOLET. (*Laughing and clinging to the hand strap.*) Slow down, Al! You're gonna kill us.

BUTCH. Shut your pie-hole, Vi. That Sheriff is hot on my bumper.

And…

BRITTANY. (*Sitting in a waiting room and muttering.*) My first audition since I hit Hollywood and what if I fail?

BRET. (*Standing in the doorway.*) Ms. Jones? We're ready for you.

And…

TONY. (*Cringing behind his desk.*) Don't read that, Mr. Nelson. The poem's not finished.

JOANIE. (*Sighing, murmurs to herself.*) He's so handsome. He doesn't even see me. I wish I was as pretty as Mary Jane.

You have an idea for a play in your mind. Write down the first idea. Write two ideas that are different. Now choose the one that is your best idea. Ideally, the first few lines of a play should capture the audience from the first utterance. This will launch your writing and your play.

Be certain that the main characters are well developed before you get too far into the dialogue (See Section 3.)

This is the chapter for 'character building and character analysis. Use this chapter to not only develop your characters but to jot down your observations of real people that you've seen and heard.

Listen to people. Notice how they speak; the cadence of their speech, the slang that they use.

I can only tell you how my stories come to me. I'm certain it's different for everyone. An idea will pop into my mind. For several days it will germinate and then it starts to write itself. When my brain is full of ideas, dialogue, and people I have to sit down at my keyboard and transfer it.

Do not feel as though you must have a whole script ready to write. I'd never get anything written if I put that kind of pressure on myself. My hope is that you find this work book/journal helpful in that way.

Now, write the first few lines of dialogue for your first or newest script here:

"A will finds a way."

Orison Swett Marden

"When I'm hungry,
I eat. When I'm
thirsty, I drink.
When I feel like
saying something,
I say it."

Madonna

> "An actor without a playwright is like a hole without a doughnut."
>
> *George Jean Nathan*

> **For those who can do it and who keep their nerve, writing for a living still beats most real, grown-up jobs hands down.**
>
> *Terence Blacker*

TIP:

I rewrite and rewrite. I love my delete key. I let magic happen. I let my characters speak to me.

> "All the world's a stage and most of us are desperately unrehearsed."
>
> *Sean O'Casey*

"A writer never has a vacation. For a writer life consists of either writing or thinking about writing."

Eugene Ionesco

> "A woman must have money and a room of her own if she is to write fiction."
>
> *Virginia Woolf*

"I don't consciously start writing a play that involves issues. After it's done, I sit back like everyone else and think about what it means."

Suzan-Lori Parks

"As a playwright, you are a torturer of actors and of the audience as well. You inflict things on people."

Tony Kushner

> **Do you know what a playwright is? A playwright is someone who lets his guts hang out on the stage.**
>
> *Edward Albee*

Don't be seduced
into thinking that
that which does
not make a profit
is without value.

Arthur Miller

> "We relish news of our heroes, forgetting that we are extraordinary to somebody too."
>
> *Helen Hayes*

"The subject of drama is The Lie. At the end of the drama THE TRUTH -- which has been overlooked, disregarded, scorned, and denied -- prevails. And that is how we know the Drama is done."

David Mamet

"A playwright must be his own audience. A novelist may lose his readers for a few pages; a playwright never dares lose his audience for a minute."

Terence Rattigan

TIP:

When I'm not writing, I'm reading. I believe, as do many other successful writers, that reading other writers inspires me to be a better writer.

> **To acquire the habit of reading is to construct for yourself a refuge from almost all the miseries of life.**
>
> *W. Somerset Maugham*

> "I want to be a playwright the way people are bank tellers. I want to keep doing it and have it go steadily and smoothly. I am constantly disappointed."

Richard Greenberg

We're all proud
of making little
mistakes. It gives
us the feeling we
don't make any
big ones.

Andy Rooney

"I like to listen. I
have learned a
great deal from
listening carefully.
Most people never
listen."

Ernest Hemingway

> **Writing is not a calling; it's a doing.**
>
> *T. Sugarek*

"You have to motivate yourself with challenges. That's how you know you're still alive."

Jerry Seinfeld

"It's an odd mix, the life of a playwright."

Laura Wade

"Be courageous and try to write in a way that scares you a little."

Holley Gerth

How to Write A Stage Play

FOURTEEN TIPS TO GET YOU STARTED

1. **Format is very important.** (See Section 8) Buy a play script or go on line to check out the approved format. When you submit your new play and it is not formatted correctly, they will not read it. There is software out there that offers auto-format. Below is a sample of the format. Notice character names are in CAPS and **bold**, followed with a period. Blocking (action) is in italics and always lower case if appearing in the 'line' of the actor. A 'beat' is a dramatic pause or to enhance the pace of the speech. There is a space between dialogue and blocking but no spaces between the lines of dialogue.

Scene One

    At Rise: A loft studio in Greenwich Village. Late afternoon. While there are many paintings it is apparent that one subject has been painted again and again. Large windows overlook the street.

        (**MONTY** *is painting at* **HIS** *easel.* **HE** *is a little paint smeared.* **HE** *hears voices from the street.*)

VOICE *(off.)*

Hey, beautiful. You're home early.

> *(Brush in one hand, palette in the other, MONTY crosses up to the windows and peers into the street below. The lilting laughter of a young woman is heard.)*

SAMANTHA *(Voice off. teasing.)*

Hey, Mr. Murray. Your wife know you're trying to pick up women in the street?

MR. MURRAY *(off.)*

No…and don't you go tellin' on me. My old woman would give me what for… bothering a young lady like you.

SAMANTHA *(Voice off.)*

Your secret is safe with me (beat.)…for a price.

MR. MURRAY *(off.)*

Oh yeah, what's that?

SAMANTHA *(off.)*

Some fresh bagels from your bakery.

MR. MURRAY *(off.)*

You got a deal. I'll bring them home with me tomorrow.

SAMANTHA *(off.)*

Thanks, Mr. Murray! I'll look forward to it. Bye, now.

MR. MURRAY *(off.)*

Bye, beautiful. See you later.

2. **Each page represents approximately one minute of time** on stage, depending upon blocking. So if you have a play that is 200 pages long, that won't work. Audiences aren't going to sit for more than one and a half hours unless you are providing a circus, a fire drill, AND an earthquake. Audiences are even reluctant to sit through "THE ICEMAN COMETH" a great classic by Eugene O'Neill. It runs close to 3

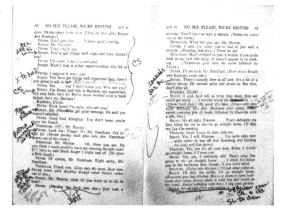

38

hours. You should keep your full length script to about 100 pages which equals 1.6 hours of stage time. For a one act divide that by 2. For a ten minute play your script should be from 10-15 pages.

3. **Leave lots of white space.** One day when your play is being produced, actors will need a place to make notes in the script during rehearsal. This is a sample of an actor's working script. An actor usually 'highlights' their lines and writes the director's blocking in the margins.

4. **The blocking** (in *italics*) is where you give the actors instructions on when and where to move. But, keep it short and sweet. Remember there will be a director who has their own ideas of where they want their actors to be. Be aware of costume changes in your writing. An actor can't exit stage left and enter stage right, seconds later, if you haven't written in the time it will take them to accomplish a costume change.

5. **Your script has to work on a stage.** (See Section 7) If your story takes place in more than one locale, you have to be aware of the logistics of a 'set' change. So keep it simple to start. If you are ambitious in your set ideas buy a book on set design to research if your set is feasible. There are some wonderful 'envelope' sets that unfold when you need to change the scene. But you have to consider the budget; would a theatre have the money to build it? Always a worry.

6. **Dialogue: Now here's the hard part:** everything you want the audience to know about the story and the characters, is conveyed in the dialogue. Unlike a short story or a novel, where you can write as much description as you'd like, a play script has none of that. NO description. For example: If it's important for the audience to know that the character is a single working parent the dialogue must weave this into the story. Another character, talking about the single parent, can be used to tell the audience this fact.

7. **Cast:** Always, always tell the reader/director/actor **how many people are in the cast**, their

gender and ages. In the beginning of your script you will have a 'character list' or Cast of Characters, stating the character's name, how they are germane to the story, and their age and physical appearance.

8. If you write a script with six to eight to ten men in it, **YOU ARE DOOMED**. Men are extremely hard to cast (they're just not out there and if they are, their jobs and families prevent them from auditioning) and so most directors are looking for a play with a reasonably small cast with more women than men. Under six to eight actors and two-thirds, women.

9. **Subject:** If this is your first play writing attempt, **write about something you know.** Maybe a family story. One of my first plays was about my days in Hollywood as an actor.

10. **Your dialogue is EVERYTHING.** You will be judged on IT alone. So try to be original, snappy, and funny. Even the most dramatic, tragic play has pathos. Be certain there are NO typo's and check your grammar. Keep asking yourself, 'Can I write it better?'

11. **The format for a stage play is entirely different from a screenplay.** Don't confuse the two. With a stage play, you are limited to what can physically be accomplished on a stage. With a screenplay you can have several locations, interior and exterior....pretty much whatever the budget will allow.

12. **Story Arc:** The end of the first act is usually the top of the story arch; keep your audience guessing during intermission so that they will not be tempted to leave during the break. Make them want to come back in to see how it all ends. Generally, the first act is longer than the second act.

13. **Terminology:** Be certain that you are well versed in theatre terminology. (See Section 8.)

Stage left, stage right, down stage, blocking, beat/s, cross, enter, exit.

14. **After you've written and rewritten your script,** get some actors together and hold a reading, to hear how your play 'sounds'. This will help you immensely with your re-writes. Invite an audience and get their feedback.

TURN THE PAGE FOR AN EXERCISE IN PLAY WRITING.

"The profession of play writing makes horse racing seem like a solid, stable business."

John Steinbeck

"In the theatre, people talk. Talk, talk until the cows come home about journeys of discovery and about what Hazlitt thought of a line of Shakespeare. I can't stand it."

Sir Anthony Hopkins

In this exercise, I have started a play for you to continue writing. It can be a 10 minute play, a full one act play, or a full length play. I have left the story plot 'threads' dangling in order for you to choose where it goes. Tip: If you choose to write a longer play you might want to consider writing something in front of these few lines to get more 'back story'. When you transfer your play to the computer, of course you will not have lines under your text. (See formatting a play. Section 8)

ACT 1
Scene 1

At Rise: A hallway in a high school.

(**JASON** and **ROBIN** stand next to some lockers away from the flow of students hurrying to their classes.)

ROBIN (Hissing.)
You better not hurt my friend.

JASON
What are you talking about?

ROBIN
I know your rep....luv 'em and leave 'em.

JASON
Naw. Not me.

ROBIN

Yes, you. Just be careful. Do not start dating Sara, coming on strong like she's the only girl in the world. Then dumping her.

JASON

I wouldn't.

ROBIN

You would. I'm just sayin', if you plan on doing something like that, you'll have to go through me to get to Sara.

JASON (Smirked.)

What if I'm planning on going through Sara to get to you?

ROBIN

What? You're crazy.

JASON

That doesn't answer my question.

ROBIN

You don't even like me.

Now finish the play....

> "There's nothing to writing. All you do is sit down at a typewriter and bleed."

Ernest Hemingway

"Love. Fall in love and stay in love. Write only what you love, and love what you write. The key word is love. You have to get up in the morning and write something you love, something to live for."

Ray Bradbury

"When you are completely absorbed or caught up in something, (writing) you become oblivious to things around you, or to the passage of time. It is this absorption in what you are doing that frees your unconscious and releases your creative imagination."

Rollo May

"Invent yourself
and then reinvent
yourself, don't swim
in the same slough.
invent yourself
and then reinvent
yourself and stay
out of the clutches
of mediocrity.
Reinvigorate
yourself and accept
what is, but only on
the terms that you
have invented and
reinvented."

Charles Bukowski

> "Always be a first-rate version of yourself, instead of a second-rate version of somebody else."
>
> *Louis L'Amour*

> **This world is but a canvas to our imagination.**
>
> *Henry Thoreau*

> Creative activity
> could be described
> as a type of learning
> process where
> teacher and pupil are
> located in the same
> individual.

Arthur Koestler

> "And in real life endings aren't always neat, whether they're happy endings, or whether they're sad endings."
>
> *Stephen King*

"Art is not a
handicraft, it is the
transmission of
feeling the artist
has experienced."

Leo Tolstoy

"Imagination grows by exercise, and contrary to common belief, is more powerful in the mature than in the young."

W. Somerset Maugham

"The reader, the book lover, must meet his own needs without paying too much attention to what his neighbors say those needs should be."

Teddy Roosevelt

TIP:

Rewrite, Rewrite, Rewrite, Rewrite and then rewrite some more. Learn to love your delete key. Not everything you write will be worthy of keeping.

The stupid believe
that to be truthful
is easy; only the
artist, the great
artist, knows how
difficult it is.

Willa Cather

> **We are what we repeatedly do. Excellence, then, is not an act, but a habit.**
>
> *Aristotle*

> Sometimes I feel like a figment of my own imagination.

Lily Tomlin

"The aim of art is to represent not the outward appearance of things, but their inward significance."

Aristotle

There's a drive in me that won't allow me to do certain things that are easy.

Johnny Depp

> **Know from whence you came. If you know whence you came, there are absolutely no limitations to where you can go.**
>
> *Tennessee Williams*

"In playwriting, you've got to be able to write dialogue. And if you write enough of it and let it flow enough, you'll probably come across something that will give you a key as to structure. I think the process of writing a play is working back and forth between the moment and the whole."

David Mamet

"An actor is something less than a man, while an actress is something more than a woman."

Richard Burton

> **What is not started today is never finished tomorrow.**
>
> *Johann Wolfgang von Goethe*

"I can take any amount of criticism as long as I can consider it unqualified praise."

Noel Coward

> **"All writers are vain, selfish, and lazy, and at the very bottom of their motives there lies a mystery. Writing a book is a horrible, exhausting struggle, like a long bout of some painful illness."**
>
> *George Orwell*

"Ideas are like
rabbits. You get a
couple and learn
how to handle them,
and pretty soon you
have a dozen."

John Steinbeck

"With any part you play, there is a certain amount of yourself in it. There has to be, otherwise it's just not acting. It's lying."

Johnny Depp

> "If you string together a set of speeches expressive of character, and well finished in point and diction and thought, you will not produce the essential tragic effect nearly so well as with a play which, however deficient in these respects, yet has a plot and artistically constructed incidents."

Aristotle

"I learned never to empty the well of my writing, but always to stop when there was still something there in the deep part of the well, and let it refill at night from the springs that fed it."

Ernest Hemingway

> Be who you are and say what you feel, because those who mind don't matter, and those who matter don't mind.

Dr. Seuss

"I think that as a playwright, if I detail that environment, then I'm taking away something from them [designers]. I'm taking away their creativity and their ability to have input themselves, not just to follow what the playwright has written. So I do a minimum set description and let the designers create within that."

August Wilson

" I hold more and more surely to the conviction that the use of masks will be discovered eventually to be the freest solution of the modern dramatist's problem as to how -- with the greatest possible dramatic clarity and economy of means -- he can express those profound hidden conflicts of the mind which the probings of psychology continue to disclose to us. "

Eugene O'Neill

"Try again. Fail again. Fail better."

Samuel Beckett

> **"I can't expose a human weakness on the stage unless I know it through having it myself."**
>
> *Tennessee Williams*

> "I don't much care for large bodies of people collected together. Everyone knows that audiences vary enormously; it's a mistake to care too much about them. The thing one should be concerned with is whether the performance has expressed what one set out to express in writing the play. It sometimes does."
>
> *Harold Pinter*

> "The Welsh people have a talent for acting that one does not find in the English. The English lack heart."
>
> *Sir Anthony Hopkins*

"Nothing you write, if you hope to be any good, will ever come out as you first hoped.

Lillian Hellman

TIP:

My journaling led me to healing, inspiration and the art of creative writing. I started writing down an idea which then became a stage play, then poetry, then books for kids. Then fiction. Write something every day.

"The script is the coloring book that you're given, and your job is to figure out how to color it in. And also when and where to color outside the lines."

James Spader

> **If you must have motivation, think of your paycheck on Friday.**
>
> *Noel Coward*

> "I may climb perhaps to no great heights, but I will climb alone."
>
> *Cyrano De-Bergerac*

"Anything you put in a play -- any speech -- has got to do one of two things: either define character or push the action of the play along."

Edward Albee

Creating Rich Characters

This chapter is dedicated to developing the characters in your play. If you don't know your characters, actors/directors/audience will never get to know them or care about them. After many years of writing, my characters show up in my head but it's my job to 'flesh them out'. Many times I will meet or see a character in real life and they will later inspire a character in my writing. But, it's still the playwright's job to give them a story and breathe life into them. If you're a new writer take the time to write it down here, using some of the tools listed. It's not the same as a few random thoughts about your character. Some intangible thing happens when you put pen to paper (or fingers to keyboard) and get to know who your character is.

First, picture the alphabet. Let's say that your character's appearance in your script is 'H' through 'M'. A good exercise that will lead you to a fully developed character is to write/create their story, 'A' through 'G'. This is their back story. Then write their story 'N' through 'Z'. (What happened to them after they leave your play.) Now you have created their entire life story. It will make your character so much more interesting.

Another great exercise for the writer: Write down and describe your character's bedroom in great detail. What kind of bedroom would your character have? What color are the walls? What's on the bed? What's hanging on the walls? What part of the house/apt is your bedroom in? What's in the closet? Is your character neat or messy? Now read it back. It should tell you much about who your character is.

Read through your script and write down EVERYTHING the other characters say about the character you are creating.

These exercises do not have to show up in your play but they will help define and add richness to your characters.

When you are editing and rewriting be certain that part of your mind is looking for additional ways to flesh out your characters. Did you tell everything about them that your readers need to know about them? Did you tie up 'loose ends' of their story as your script progressed.

Explore your characters' motivations, goals, needs.

Villains versus Heroes: Heroes are easy to write. Your protagonist is honorable, friendly, good and kind. Villains not so much. There should be something that the reader can like about the antagonist. Perhaps it's a cutting wit. Maybe an act of kindness or something your audience can at least empathize with. Maybe it's something as simple as they are kind to their mother.

Using some of these tools try writing a character description/analysis here:

_____

_____

_____

_____

_____

_____

_____

_____

_____

_____

_____

_____

> Intelligence
> without ambition
> is a bird without
> wings.

Salvador Dali

TIP:

Go to a local park, a ball game, a church, a bar, a grocery store, (you get the idea) and watch people.

> "There are nights when the wolves are silent and only the moon howls."
>
> *George Carlin*

> Between two evils,
> I always pick the
> one I never tried
> before.

Mae West

Don't look forward
to the day you
stop suffering,
because when it
comes you'll know
you're dead.

Tennessee Williams

"If you practice an art, be proud of it and make it proud of you. It may break your heart, but it will fill your heart before it breaks it; it will make you a person in your own right."

Maxwell Anderson

"Love is the one emotion actors allow themselves to believe."

James Spader

"When I was a boy, I always saw myself as a hero in comic books and in movies. I grew up believing this dream."

Elvis Presley

"I'm not funny.
What I am
is brave."

Lucille Ball

> "Every secret of a writer's soul, every experience of his life, every quality of his mind is written large in his works."
>
> *Virginia Woolf*

> **When I played drunks I had to remain sober because I didn't know how to play them when I was drunk.**
>
> *Richard Burton*

> "Life is one grand, sweet song, so start the music."
>
> *Ronald Reagan*

> "The real reason for comedy is to hide the pain."
>
> *Wendy Wasserstein*

> "Hope is the feeling that the feeling you have isn't permanent."
>
> *Jean Kerr*

> **If you ask people what they've always wanted to do, most people haven't done it. That breaks my heart.**
>
> *Angelina Jolie*

> "If you took acting away from me, I'd stop breathing."
>
> *Ingrid Bergman*

> "It isn't what I do, but how I do it. It isn't what I say, but how I say it, and how I look when I do it and say it."
>
> *Mae West*

TIP:

You can create an amalgam of two or three different people; take traits that you want to use from each one; mining for gold.

> **Love yourself first and everything else falls into line. You really have to love yourself to get anything done in this world.**
>
> *Lucille Ball*

"The term 'serious actor' is kind of an oxymoron, isn't it? Like 'Republican party' or 'airplane food."

Johnny Depp

> "Acting is a nice childish profession - pretending you're someone else and, at the same time, selling yourself."
>
> *Katherine Hepburn*

> "Be yourself. The world worships the original."
>
> *Ingrid Bergman*

> **The most important thing in acting is honesty. If you can fake that, you've got it made.**
>
> *George Burns*

> "If you do not tell the truth about yourself you cannot tell it about other people.
>
> *Virginia Woolf*

> "If you want to be successful, it's just this simple. Know what you are doing. Love what you are doing. And believe in what you are doing."

Will Rogers

> **The run I was on made Sinatra, Flynn, Jagger, Richards, all of them look like droopy-eyed armless children.**
>
> *Charlie Sheen*

"The whole difference between construction and creation is exactly this: that a thing constructed can only be loved after it is constructed; but a thing created is loved before it exists."

Charles Dickens

"I am able to
play monsters
well. I
understand
monsters. I
understand
madmen.**"**

Sir Anthony Hopkins

"You are never so alone as when you are ill on stage. The most nightmarish feeling in the world is suddenly to feel like throwing up in front of four thousand people."

Judy Garland

"When writing a novel a writer should create living people; people not characters. A character is a caricature."

Ernest Hemingway

> "There are three primary urges in human beings; food, sex and rewriting someone else's play."

Romulus Linney

"Well, Art is Art, isn't it? Still, on the other hand, water is water. And east is east and west is west and if you take cranberries and stew them like applesauce they taste much more like prunes than rhubarb does. Now you tell me what you know."

Groucho Marx

> "As kids we're not taught how to deal with success; we're taught how to deal with failure. If at first you don't succeed, try, try again. If at first you succeed, then what?"

Charlie Sheen

"Some of my best leading men have been dogs and horses."

Elizabeth Taylor

TIP:

Take from real life whenever you can. The most fascinating characters are real people.

> "I don't go by the rule book... I lead from the heart, not the head."
>
> *Princess Diana*

"If I give my characters free will, if I don't plot out the story and instead present them with a problem and watch them deal with it, they begin to take on a life of their own, frequently surprising me with the choices they make."

Dean Koontz

"The theater is so endlessly fascinating because it's so accidental. It's so much like life."

Arthur Miller

Story Telling

If play writing is a new project for you it will take some practice to tell your 'story' with dialogue.

Part of the story will be told by the appearance of your characters; hair styles, costumes, etc. The set, if there is one, will tell part of the story. But nothing tells the story and moves it along like the dialogue.

On the following pages you might try writing a short story. Keep it about some people and a story line you already know. I suggest a short story/play to begin with. Maybe about the Thanksgiving dinner last year and your crazy uncle. Maybe about a family reunion and your cousin coming out. Perhaps the last book club you attended. A scandal at your church. See? It can be about anything.

Now, using the voices of your characters in your story try converting your story into dialogue and only dialogue. If, when you go back and read it, the dialogue doesn't move the story forward but tells the audience something pertinent about a character - keep it. If the dialogue does neither - use the good old 'delete' key.

If you are going to self-publish (with any number of platforms out there) start writing your story using a blank template that the platform offers. **This saves you a lot of time formatting your play after the fact.** Here's a good self-publishing platform:

https://kdp.amazon.com/en_US/help?query=paperback+templates. But I digress.

Your script will now take shape and you can concentrate on your story. The dialogue should resemble how real people speak. Few of us speak the 'King's English'. If you are an American playwright, telling a story about Americans (or nationals) your dialogue should sound authentic. Of course the future actors speaking your dialogue will hopefully take care of this for you. I wrote a play about an Indian family running a bodega. While my dialogue didn't mimic the Indian accent, I tried to infuse it with that certain cadence in which Indian people speak English. Then I left it to the actors.

One thing you will see in almost all scripts is conflict. An obstacle that a character/s must overcome.

Then there is subjective expectations meets objective realty. Another strong conflict. In a full length play you have time to create a beginning, middle and end. But in a short play think more in terms of Normal-Explosion-New normal.

Another tactic is story delaying. Ask dramatic questions (figuratively). Will the character live? Will the king forgive his son? Will the guy get the girl? Drag out the solution. But of course, with play writing, you only have a hundred pages in which to do it.

Your audience wants to learn life's lessons without have to go through the pain of the lesson.

Make your story dramatic. If the story is boring, nobody cares. You can exaggerate; make the situation a life or death situation even if it isn't.

Your first attempts at telling a story doesn't have to set the world ablaze. Just a simple story to get you started so that you can practice telling it in the form of dialogue. Try writing some dialogue now.

> "Language is wine upon the lips."
>
> *Virginia Woolf*

"Cock your hat -
angles are attitudes."

Frank Sinatra

> "You can design and create, and build the most wonderful place in the world. But it takes people to make the dream a reality.

Walt Disney

"When I first started writing plays I couldn't write good dialogue because I didn't respect how black people talked. I thought that in order to make art out of their dialogue I had to change it, make it into something different. Once I learned to value and respect my characters, I could really hear them. I let them start talking."

August Wilson

"Truth is like the sun. You can shut it out for a time, but it ain't goin' away."

Elvis Presley

"What is life but a series of inspired follies? The difficulty is to find them to do."

George Bernard Shaw

> "A playwright is the litmus paper of the arts. He's got to be, because if he isn't working on the same wave length as the audience, no one would know what in hell he was talking about."
>
> *Arthur Miller*

> **You can observe a lot by just watching.**
>
> *Yogi Berra*

"The way to get started is to quit talking and begin doing."

Walt Disney

I honestly think it is better to be a failure at something you love than to be a success at something you hate.

George Burns

> **Don't let yesterday use up too much of today.**
>
> *Will Rogers*

"The person who says it cannot be done should not interrupt the person doing it."

Chinese Proverb

"What shouldn't you do if you're a young playwright? Don't bore the audience! I mean, even if you have to resort to totally arbitrary killing on stage, or pointless gunfire, at least it'll catch their attention and keep them awake. Just keep the thing going any way you can."

Tennessee Williams

> "I had no desire to be an film actress, to always play somebody else, to be always beautiful with somebody constantly straightening out your every eyelash. It was always a big bother to me."
>
> *Marlene Dietrich*

> "There is a crack in
> everything, that's
> how the light gets in."
>
> *Leonard Cohen*

"The last collaborator is your audience ... when the audience comes in, it changes the temperature of what you've written. Things that seem to work well -- work in a sense of carry the story forward and be integral to the piece -- suddenly become a little less relevant or a little less functional or a little overlong or a little overweight or a little whatever. And so you start reshaping from an audience."

Stephen Sondheim

> "One usually dislikes a play while writing it, but afterward it grows on one. Let others judge and make decisions."

Anton Chekhov

"A conflict in a book is a situation or meeting between characters that results in challenge and opposition. Conflict, such as a power struggle between a hero (or protagonist) and villain (or antagonist) is arguably the most important element in fiction because without conflict there is no movement and no narrative drive."

Nownovel.com

Plot, Protagonist, Antagonist, Conflict

As a playwright you better find some conflict in your story. Little Women had soft, cozy conflict but make no mistake there is conflict. Romeo and Juliet had glaring conflict represented by a family feud that wrought murder and mayhem. To be successful, you must have antagonists and protagonists in your plot.

CONFLICT: It is a challenge to write conflict with dialogue only. There is no description (like fiction) where you can tell the reader how angry and against something your antagonist is. Granted you have the characters right there in front of you, to tell the story with their body language but the dialogue carries the day and is the difference between weak writing and strong, successful writing.

Using examples from a recent play of mine, I will demonstrate conflict in simple, but successful (to the overall plot of the play) terms. A children's play but the rules still apply and are no less challenging because it's a kids' play.

Sub-PLOT: The sooner the plot is revealed the better. If you haven't engaged the audience in the first three minutes, you don't have a very good plot. In Emma and the Aardvarks the plot begins on the first page of script. Two Aardvarks, sisters, tumble out of a Time Portal and into the fabled forest. In minutes the occupants of the forest discover them and the audience discovers the protagonists and antagonists.

Example: (Plot) On page one we have established the beginning of a plot: two Aardvarks lost in a strange forest.

AGNES ©

I think we're lost, dear sister. This doesn't look anything like the pictures of Australia in our book.

ANNIE

Oh, dear, I'm quite afraid.

STARE

Who?

ANNIE

Ekk. What was that?

AGNES

What?

ANNIE

That. I don't like this place, Agnes.

AGNES

You're such a scaredy-cat, Annie. It's a simple forest, much like the jungles of home.

DONALD
(Enters.)

Hello. Don't go. I mean you no harm.

With the dialogue, we've told the audience that the two sisters are in the forest by accident. That their destination had been Australia. They meet their first friend (protagonist.

ANTAGONISTS: We'll return to the plot later but let's go on...Enter the first antagonist. This character is very selfish and immediately is suspicious of the two newcomers.

Example: (Antagonist)

PATSY (Banana Spider)
(Knitting her web very fast.)

Eye--eee! Por favor, who are these ugly newcomers? Dios mío, ¿se comerán mis insectos? The bugs are for me and me alone!

DONALD (Fairie)

Patsy, where are your manners? Everyone is welcome in the fabled forest, as long as they come in peace.

PATSY

Dios mio, how do we know they come in peace, pequeño? Se ven como bandidos!

A Protagonist enters:

EMMA (Earthling)
Please join us. Donald introduce us immediately.

DONALD

Miss Agnes, Miss Annie, this is my friend, Emma.

EMMA

Oh! You are so cute. It's nice to meet new friends. And such pretty hats. May I? *(EMMA reached up and adjusted the frothy thing atop AGNES' head that had been knocked askew in the mad dash into the forest.)* You're the shy young lady, aren't you? May I adjust your hat, Miss Annie? There! All fixed. May I ask? What species are you?

PLOT: *After a few main characters are established, we continue to weave the main Plot, (all told through dialogue) which is about global warming and endangered species.*

Example (Plot):

EMMA

Miss Agnes, why were you going to Australia?

AGNES

Back home, in Africa, we are losing our habitat to humans, farms, and roads.

ANNIE

It's terrible. There aren't very many of us aardvarks left, you know.

CHEETS (Elf)

What does that mean? 'Not many of you left'?

AGNES

We're being killed off.

EMMA

Oh no! But you're so cute. And if you're insectivores, you help keep the natural world balanced.

AGNES

One would think so. *(Beat.)* So when our habitat goes, we go. We are threatened.

ANTAGONISTS & PROTAGONISTS: The Plot thickens when you have more than one antagonist *and protagonist.*

Example (Antagonist and Protagonists.):

CHEETS

I don't like them. Nope. Don't like the look of them and they smell funny.

(A simple statement: 'I don't like them.' But highly effective.)

STARE (Owl)

Who?

CHEETS

Those two, whad-ya-call-ems.

EMMA

Aardvarks.

CHEETS

Yeah☐them.

EMMA

Cheets, that's unkind. You know nothing of Annie and Agnes. They seem perfectly fine to me. In fact, I think they're cute.

THOMAS (Sea Turtle)

Those two ladies are my friends from the Dark Continent. *(To Cheets.)* As for you, you, you scurvy young scallywag you keep yer opinions to yerself.

CHEETS

But what if they eat someone we know?

EMMA

Cheets, that's silly. Do you know any ants? Beetles? Termites on a personal basis?

CHEETS

Noooo, but I might meet some.

EMMA

Yes, Cheets, you're judging these newcomers and deciding you don't like them based on what? Nothing.

CHEETS

Don't care. Still don't like 'em. Who ever heard of aardvarks, anyway?

CONFLICT:
5 Ways to Create Conflict in Your Story:

Give your characters clear goals.

Go big, go small.

Let your characters fail.

Make your characters opinionated.

Use exposition to your advantage.

The Time Portal is malfunctioning. Some of the occupants of the forest are welcoming, some are suspicious and angry.

Example:

EMMA

He's very excitable, Miss Agnes. Are you really from Africa?

ANNIE

Yes, Miss Emma, we were going on vacation and then this happened.

EMMA

Oh, dear, I'm sorry.

AGNES

Yes, our travel agent, Time Portal for All Your Vacation Needs, was supposed to send us to Australia. We have distant relatives there. Something must have gone wrong. Someone at the agency pushed the wrong button.

ANNIE

Where are we, exactly?

CHEETS

You're in the Fabled Forest. Don't you know anything?

AGNES

Who raised you? Dogs? No, not dogs, they are strict with their children. Hyenas, perhaps? Yes, hyenas, our arch enemies.

More CONFLICT:

Example:

EMMA
(To the dogs.)

Welcome to our forest. I am Emma and these are my friends. Where did you come from?

AGNES

Emma, you don't want to be friends with them. After all they're just dogs.

Remember, dialog is simply conversation between your characters. In your story, imagine what your characters would say to each other. The more conflict you create in your story, the richer the story will be. Be aware of 'loose ends' when you're solving the conflict.

Note*: The character description next to names is meant only for this exercise and is NOT used when formatting your play.*

"Get into the scene
late, get out of the
scene early."

David Mamet

"Get your facts first,
then you can distort
them as you please."

Mark Twain

"I'm a writer. The more I act, the more resistance I have to it. If you accept work in a movie, you accept to be entrapped for a certain part of time, but you know you're getting out. I'm also earning enough to keep my horses, buying some time to write."

Sam Shepard

> **There is just one life for each of us: our own.**
>
> *Euripedes*

"The apple cannot be stuck back on the Tree of Knowledge; once we begin to see, we are doomed and challenged to seek the strength to see more, not less.

Arthur Miller

> **If** history were taught in the form of stories, it would never be forgotten.
>
> *Rudyard Kipling*

> "I restore myself when I'm alone."
>
> *Marilyn Monroe*

"In a play, from the beginning, you have to realize that you're preparing something which is going into the hands of other people, unknown at the time you're writing it."

T. S. Eliot

"New dramatic writing has banished conversational dialogue from the stage as a relic of dramaturgy based on conflict and exchange: any story, intrigue or plot that is too neatly tied up is suspect."

Patrice Pavis

"I get fed up with all this nonsense of ringing people up and lighting cigarettes and answering the doorbell that passes for action in so many modern plays."

Graham Greene

> Fiction is like
> a spider's web,
> attached ever so
> slightly perhaps,
> but still attached
> to life at all four
> corners. Often
> the attachment
> is scarcely
> perceptible.
>
> *Virginia Woolf*

> "To have great
> stories, there
> must be great
> audiences too."
>
> *Walt Whitman*

> Start writing, no matter what. The water does not flow until the faucet is turned on.
>
> *Louis L'Amour*

> "Write hard and clear about what hurts."

Ernest Hemingway

> "The thing all writers do best is find ways to avoid writing."
>
> *Alan Dean Foster*

> "You can always edit a bad page. You can't edit a blank page."
>
> *Jodi Picoult*

> "To me, the greatest pleasure of writing is not what it's about, but the inner music that words make."
>
> *Truman Capote*

"The art of the dramatist is very like the art of the architect. A plot has to be built up just as a house is built-- story after story; and no edifice has any chance of standing unless it has a broad foundation and a solid frame."

Brander Matthews

> "Writing has ... been to me like a bath from which I have risen feeling cleaner, healthier, and freer."

Henrik Ibsen

> Some people see things that are and ask, Why? Some people dream of things that never were and ask, Why not? Some people have to go to work and don't have time for all that.

George Carlin

"I love writing. I love the swirl and swing of words as they tangle with human emotion."

James Michener

> "When asked, 'How do you write?' I invariably answer, 'one word at a time.'"
>
> *Stephen King*

"I wish I could write as mysterious as a cat."

Edgar Allan Poe

"Oh! Do not attack me with your watch. A watch is always too fast or too slow. I cannot be dictated to by a watch."

Jane Austen

> Dreams are illustrations... from the book your soul is writing about you.

Marsha Norman

> "Good novels are not written, they are rewritten. Great novels are diamonds mined from layered rewrites."
>
> *Andre Jute*

"Writing is supposed to be difficult, agonizing, a dreadful exercise, a terrible occupation."

Ray Bradbury

> "The place where you made your stand never mattered. Only that you were there... and still on your feet."
>
> *Stephen King*

> "I think that's foolishness on the part of the playwright to write about himself. People don't know anything about themselves."
>
> *Edward Albee*

"Whenever I'm asked what advice I have for young writers, I always say that the first thing is to read, and to read a lot. The second thing is to write. And the third thing, which I think is absolutely vital, is to tell stories and listen closely to the stories you're being told."

John Green

How to Block

Many playwrights never write a single line of blocking in the script. After all, that's the director's vision and job. I am one of those who writes a moderate amount of blocking in the script even knowing that the director may change it at will.

It is so engrained in me as a director/playwright to write what I 'see' in my mind's eye. But if you do write in blocking, be certain to use the proper theatre terminology. (See Section 9.)

A few do's and don'ts:

(Blocking is written in parentheses, italics, and indented.) Examples are written throughout this workbook.

Never have your actors in a straight line on stage unless you are writing "Chorus Line".

Groups of three are ideal if you have 4 or more actors in your scene.

When writing your blocking it should be written as exampled in section 9. Have your character 'move' before or after their line; never during.

(*The* **STUDENTS** *are waiting for their teacher.*
There's not a lot of noise in the room
as the **STUDENTS** *are glued to their mobile devices*
tapping away. **MS. ELLIS** *enters.*)

(**BRANDON** *and* **LILY** *cross reluctantly to a pair of chairs.*
THEY stand by a chair, not making eye contact.)

(**TOM** *crawls back to* **HIS** *desk, but stays on the floor.*)

"I love working
with a set designer
because, in many
respects, you meet
the set designer
before you meet
the actors. So it's
a chance for me
as a director to
figure out what
I'm thinking and
to explore how
the space is going
to actually be
activated."

George C. Wolfe

> "Nothing matters but the writing. There has been nothing else worthwhile...a stain upon the silence."
>
> *Samuel Beckett*

" Make another failure like that... and you'll be immortal. "

Balzac

"The mission of the playwright is to look in his heart and write, to write whatever concerns him at the moment; to write with passion and conviction. Of course the measure of the man will be the measure of the play."

Robert Anderson

Snappy Dialogue

Hopefully you have read a few scripts. It is imperative to read at least a few to get an idea of format, what clean and snappy dialogue looks like. It will get your brain used to seeing the correct format, how a conversation (dialogue) flows and how the dialogue tells you, the actor, and the audience everything they need to know about the character who is speaking or the character they are speaking to or about. For example: In Simon's play, California Suite:

ACT ONE (Note: The format is not what we use currently. But see how well Simon tells you about a character through his dialogue for another character.)

HANNAH Oh, that should be fun. Something like the Universal Studio tour?

BILLY What a snob you are.

HANNAH Thank God there's a few of us left ..

BILLY What is there so beautiful about your life that makes it so important to put down everyone else's?

Forty square blocks bounded by Lincoln Center on the west and Cinema II on the east is not the center of the goddamn universe. I grant you it's an exciting, vibrant, stimulating, fabulous city, but it is not Mecca. • • It just smells like it.

HANNAH The hell with New York! Or Boston or Washington or Philadelphia. I don't care where Jenny lives, but how. She's an intelligent girl with a good mind. Let it grow and prosper.

But what the hell is she going to learn in a community that has valet parking just to pick up four bagels and the Hollywood Reporter?

BILLY I've been to Martha's Vineyard in July, Hannah. Heaven protect me from another intellectual Cape Cod summer. . . The political elite queueing up in old beach sandals to see Bogart pictures, standing there eating ice cream cones and reading the New Republic.

HANNAH Neat, wasn't it?

BILLY No. Your political friends never impressed me. I remember one hot Sunday afternoon in Hyannis port when our ambassador to some war-torn Middle Eastern country was in a state of despair because he couldn't get the hang of throwing a Frisbee. My God, the absurdity.

Another sample of how Tennessee Williams (Streetcar) tells the story through dialogue:

> BLANCHE. I need to be near you, Stella; I've got to be witb people, I *can't* be alone!
> Because-as you must have noticed-I'm-not very *well!* (*Her voice drops, her look* is *frightened.*)
> STELLA. (*Rises, Crosses* to R. of BLANCHE, *places hand on her shoulder.*) You seem a little bit nervous or overwrought or some-thing.
> BLANCHE. Will Stanley like me, or will I be just a visiting in-law? I couldn't stand that, Stella. (::*Turns* to STELLA.)
> STELLA. (*Turns* to BLANCHE.) You'll get along fine together, if you'll just try not to-well-compare him with men we went out with at home.
> BLANCHE. Is he so--different?
> STELLA. Yes. A different species.
> BLANCHE. In what way; what's he like?
> STELLA. Oh, you can't describe someone you're in love with. (*She crosses above BLANCHE to dressing-table, picks up photo of STANLEY, which, in a small frame, bas a place of honor on table. BLANCHE crosses in to above armchair, and when STELLA turns to BLANCHE with photo, she sits in chair, facing upstage.*) Here's a picture of him!

BLANCHE. (*Taking photo.*) An officer?

STELLA. A Master Sergeant in the Engineers' Corps. Those are decorations!

BLANCHE. He must have had those on when you met him?

STELLA. I assure you I wasn't just blinded by all the brass. But of course there were things to adjust myself to later on.

BLANCHE. Such as his civilian background! How did he take it when you told him I was coming?

STELLA. Oh, Stanley doesn't know yet.

BLANCHE. (*Frightened.*) You-haven't told him?

STELLA. He's on the road a good deal.

BLANCHE. Oh. He travels?

STELLA. Yes.

BLANCHE. I mean-isn't it?

STELLA. (*Takes photo.*) I can hardly stand it when he's away for a night ...

BLANCHE. Why, Stella!

STELLA. When he's away for a week, I nearly go wild!

BLANCHE. (*Crossing* u. L.) Gracious!

Now try some dialogue of your own. List your characters on a page and then write dialogue for them. Remember you want to tell something about the character speaking, or, move the story forward or, tell something about the other character/s.

"And by the way, everything in life is writable about if you have the outgoing guts to do it, and the imagination to improvise. The worst enemy to creativity is self-doubt."

Sylvia Plath

> "Good scripts are not written, they are rewritten. Great scripts are diamonds mined from layered rewrites.
>
> *Andre Jute*

> "Promise me you'll always remember: You're braver than you believe and stronger than you seem, and smarter than you think."

A.A. Milne

> The desire to write grows with writing.
>
> *Desiderius Erasmus*

> " I must write it all
> out at any cost.
> Writing is thinking.
> It is more than
> living, for it is being
> conscious of living. "

Anne Morrow Lindbergh

> "As a writer you try to listen to what others aren't saying...and write about the silence."
>
> *N. R. Hart*

> "Step into a scene and let it drip from your fingertips."
>
> *MJ Bush*

> We write to taste life twice. In the moment and in retrospect.

Anais Nin

"An opening line should invite the reader to begin the story. It should say: Listen. Come in here. You want to know about this."

Stephen King

> " I think new writers are too worried that it has all been said before. Sure it has but not by you. "

Asha Dornfest

> "Just say the lines and don't trip over the furniture."
>
> *Noel Coward*

> "That's what storytellers do. We restore order with imagination. We instill hope again and again."
>
> *Tom Hanks*

> "Acting is a great way to make a living, especially when I consider what my alternatives were and probably still are..."
>
> *James Spader*

"The theatre is the only institution in the world which has been dying for four thousand years and has never succumbed. It requires tough and devoted people to keep it alive."

John Steinbeck

"Acting touches nerves you have absolutely no control over."

Alan Rickman

210

> **"I love acting.
> It is so much
> more real
> than life."**
>
> *Oscar Wilde*

"Playwrights are naturally wary and protective - God, who's more protective than a playwright? You read a play, the playwright wants to hear from you immediately."

Gene Saks

Set Design

Most theatres have a set designer who creates the set based on the director's vision. But it is important that the playwright sees the set. Where your story takes place. If your set requires two different scenes/sets and you have structured the play around two sets you must think about time and money. Anticipate the cost because you want the director to choose your play to produce. But if the cost of more than one set is too much, your play might never be chosen.

An envelope design works nicely for the need of two locations/sets in one play. The first set in created on the outside fold of an envelope. When the scene changes the 'flap' is opened, like a tri-fold (by the stage crew) and a new set/location is used. Set pieces (Furnishings) have to be changed out and this calls for some cleverness on the director's part.

One play comes to mind that I directed: The Cemetery Club. The main set was a living room of one of the female characters. But I also needed a Jewish cemetery. The four widows went there every month to visit their dead husbands and maintain the gravesite.

So what I designed was a single backdrop (scenery). What you might see out the living room window. Then I furnished the living room with set pieces. Sofa, chairs, coffee table, lamps, etc.

Upstage on a riser I created the cemetery with three graves. I designed star foam monuments with the Star of David on the downstage side. The women would walk up on the risers and, while gazing at the graves, deliver their monologues. It worked because the actors believed it. Thus the audience believed it.

Another set design was a real challenge: Cheatin' was three locations: a sleazy motel room, a western bar and a beauty salon. With a very tight budget. And no breaks between set changes. So I put all three locations on the stage together. Not one audience member complained about it and it won best set design that year.

I have seen productions where the set was two risers painted black (Othello). And it worked because the actors believed it.

I saw an Irish play in Dublin where the entire set was a series of doors, stage right and left and upstage. That's all the story needed.

I was in a play by Peter Weiss, The Investigation where I shared 30 roles with 7 other actors. The entire set was different size and shape boxes that were moved around. From Nazi internment camps to a war-crime court room, it worked.

It is 'Suspension of Disbelief'

The temporary acceptance as believable of events or characters that would ordinarily be seen as incredible. This is usually to allow an audience to appreciate works of literature or drama that are exploring unusual ideas.

Well designed and placed lighting can effect a scene change. Far downstage, left stands a small table with a lamp and a phone on it. A spotlight comes up on the actor and you are transported to another place.

Following are unlined, blank pages for set design. Try designing a set or two. It can be rough. Remember no one is going to see it but you!

"I wanted to be a set designer when I was young.

Judi Dench

"Art is not what you see, but what you make others see.

Edgar Degas

"A bookstore is one of the only pieces of evidence we have that people are still thinking."

Jerry Seinfeld

"Good set design is like a refrigerator—when it works, no one notices, but when it doesn't, it sure stinks."

Irene Au

"There are darknesses in life and there are lights, and you are one of the lights, the light of all lights."

Bram Stoker, *Dracula*

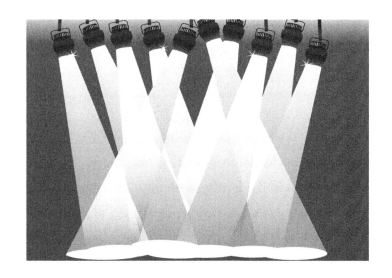

Lighting Design

Back in the day when there were truly 'starving actors' we did start up theatre companies all the time with a couple of platforms and four 'spots' that one would use in a shop in the garage at home.

This is a cheap ($12. a piece) adaptable, portable light. You can even attach a gel to the cone for a few pennies per gel. Use blues for night and warm colors (amber) for day.

Each light has a wire running back to the control desk/booth and while you won't have a dimmer option, you must be able to turn the light off and on.

When we started our own company, we had to be totally portable as our performance space could be an art gallery, a café, a gymnasium, or school auditorium. Anywhere they would allow us to use their space. All sites had to be vacated when the weekend was over and then loaded back in for the next performance date.

We could light just about any play with four of these clamp-on, shop lights. The purpose of any stage lighting is to light the actors and the set. If you don't accomplish anything else, you need to make certain this happens. If your stage is in a very small space, it's not super critical to light the actors brightly. Just be certain they stay in the light, which is where the director's blocking comes in.

Even if you need to stick to the basics of simple illumination, lighting makes everything feel more professional and helps the audience to better focus on what is going on, on the stage. Theatrical lighting doesn't have to be overly complicated. Lighting is about making certain that you can see the people on stage and that the moods of the play are represented and amplified. Clamp lights aren't the be all and end all. You'll have to live with the shadows that they cast. But remember, this is all you can afford now, and you'll also need to be able to break it down and take the lighting with you.

I still remember the thrill when we could finally afford a couple of Klieg lights.

 You can attach a 'Gobo' to the Klieg that creates a silhouette (on the back flat) of trees, a city skyline, seasonal leaves falling, etc. I lit a one woman show (*Scent of Magnolia*) with four Kliegs and four Gobos creating a ghetto, a big city, a back alley, etc.

 Klieg lighting is generally fixed for each show. You have general lighting for the stage, you might have one Klieg dedicated to a scene/location inside the scene. When you have a control board you will be able to dim your lights or bring them up to their highest setting. The stage should always be brighter than the audience area. Ideally your audience is in total darkness.

Lighting Boards: When you buy your first control board, you should look at your needs today; how many klieg-like lights do you have, is the installation permanent or do you still have to do a load-out after the last weekend performance. Now look ahead and see if the board you are considering has the capacity to serve your needs three or five years down the road. Don't over buy.

I leave you with this: With one platform, five boxes, (for a set) and five clamp lights we won the city-wide best play award in New Orleans for *The Investigation*. It wasn't perfect, we were crammed into a small art gallery in the French Quarter. Our sold-out audience numbered sixty-five seats every night. But we got our actors lit and they did the rest!

". . . a new play by Peter Weiss, acclaimed author of Marat/Sade . . ."

"The baby bat
Screamed out in fright,
'Turn on the dark,
I'm afraid of the light."

Shel Silverstein

To shine your brightest light is to be who you truly are.

Roy T. Bennett

“No one lights a lamp in order to hide it behind the door: the purpose of light is to create more light, to open people’s eyes, to reveal the marvels around.”

Paulo Coelho

> "We can easily forgive a child who is afraid of the dark; the real tragedy of life is when men are afraid of the light."
>
> *Plato*

> "If a man is to shed the light of the sun upon other men, he must first of all have it within himself."
>
> *Romain Rolland*

"A room is like a stage. If you see it without lighting, it can be the coldest place in the world."

Paul Lynde

"In theatre, the playwright is the boss, period. The decisions will go through him or her. In movies, the writer is pretty far down on the list."

Tracy Letts

Formatting Your Play

It's important to know that the correct way to format a stage play for submitting (to a publisher, agent or theatre) is very different from the format used when self-publishing it. Below is a sample of the correct formatting.

Formatting: ACT number in caps; Scene in lower caps, centered. Blocking (action) is 1 indent in and in parentheses, Character's name in caps and centered. If blocking is one word or one line it is placed on the same line as the Character's name. If longer it is on the next line in parenthesis.

Title Page (first page) of your script: Play title and Playwright's name. Add contact info on this page if you are submitting to a publisher, agent or theatre.

On the first few pages of the script book, list the Cast of Characters. Characters' names are in caps. Place and Time are below the list of characters or on the next page. Sample:

Cast of characters *(place near the front of the book. On the 3rd or 4th page after title, playwright's name, copyright notices.etc.)*

Emilee. Age 13, a pubescent girl making decisions

Danny. Age 14, emilee's first boyfriend

Maribeth. Age 22, emilee's older sister

Emilee's best friends
Ruth. Age 13. The timid one
Barb. Age 14. The bold one
Sue.   Age 14. The worrier

Setting

A park bench. Middle school. Emilee's house.

Time

Present day.

Format sample: *(From my published short play, "No means No!"©) the formatting of the dramatist play service (publishers) do use parentheses when formatting the blocking. It is jumbled into dialogue even though it does not pertain to that particular character's 'action'. I find this very distracting but i am certain it has to do with production costs and keeping the page count down. Blocking direction is indented, italicized and in parentheses. Character's names are all in caps and not italicized. Before dialogue, characters' names are all in caps with a period. Blocking is indented. Scene breaks should be on the next (right) page. There are no extra line-spaces between blocking and dialogue except if there is a 'beat' when the same character pauses. Be certain to leave plenty of white space for the actors/director's written notes. I prefer the format used by (my publisher) Samuel French, Inc. Which you see below:*

Scene 1

At Rise: A neighborhood park near a middle school. Midafternoon.

(**EMILEE** *and* **DANNY** *are seated upstage on a bench, with their backs to the audience.*)

EMILEE *(interrupting their kiss.)*

No! Cut it out Danny.

(**EMILEE** *rises turns downstage.* **DANNY** *rises.*)

DANNY

I want you, Em. Stop being such a tease.

EMILEE

I don't want to. I'm not ready.

　　(**SHE** *crosses further down.*)

You're going too fast. I don't want to.

　　　　　　DANNY (*Crosses to her, kneads her shoulders.*)

I thought you loved me.

EMILEE

I do.

DANNY

　　(**HIS** *hands start to slowly descend toward her chest.*)

Okay then.

　　　　　　EMILEE (*Pushing him away.*)

Stop it! I said 'no'.

　　(**EMILEE** *breaks away and exits.*)

DANNY

Em! Come back. I love you.

(End of sample)

Following are lots of pages for you to try writing in the correct format.

"Planning to write is not writing. Outlining a book is not writing. Researching is not writing. Talking to people about what you're doing is not writing. None of that is writing. Writing is writing."

E.L. Doctorow

I regard the theatre as the greatest of all art forms, the most immediate way in which a human being can share with another the sense of what it is to be a human being.

Oscar Wilde

"Talent will get you in the door,
but character will keep you in the room."

Unknown

"Theatre is a sacred space for actors. You are responsible; you are in the driving seat."

Greta Scacchi

> **I have only one rule in acting. Trust the director and give him heart and soul.**
>
> *Ava Gardner*

> "Theatre is not a state of being... but a state of appearing to be."

Noel Coward

> "The purpose of a rehearsal is to learn everyone else's part...never your own. Your own preparation is your welcoming gift to your colleagues."

Unknown

> "Paris is the playwright's delight. New York is the home of directors. London, however, is the actor's city, the only one in the world. In London actors are given their head."

Orson Welles

> "One is just an interpreter of what the playwright thinks, and therefore the greater the playwright, the more satisfying it is to act in the plays."
>
> *Vivien Leigh*

> "If you leave the room making the director excited and inspired, they will want more of that feeling...and that's when they cast you."
>
> *Mae Ross*

TIP:

Be certain that your grammar and spelling are impeccable. Nothing distracts a reader, an editor or a theatre (that might consider your work) more than glaring spelling and grammatical errors.

> "The person, be it gentleman or lady, who has not pleasure in a good novel, must be intolerably stupid."

Jane Austen

> "There's no American playwright after 1945 who wasn't profoundly affected - who didn't have their DNA changed by Tennessee Williams."

John Guare

> "An actor without techies is a naked person standing in the dark trying to emote.
> A techie without actors is a person with marketable skills."

Unknown

> **We are all born mad. Some remain so.**
>
> *Samuel Beckett*

> If you were to say to me that I couldn't paint, I would write. If I couldn't write, I would be a set designer. As long as I'm creating something, I'm happy.

Grace Slick

It's the actors who are prepared to make fools of themselves who are usually the ones who come to mean something to the audience.

Christian Bale

> "I loved putting on stories as plays when I was just six. I was the director, the actress and the set designer; I cast my girlfriends in parts, and I suggested to the local kindergarten teachers that we do free performances for the children."
>
> *Mili Avital*

> "Movies will make
> you famous,
> television will make
> you rich, but theatre
> will make you good."
>
> *Terrance Mann*

> My working habits are simple: long periods of thinking, short periods of writing.

Ernest Hemingway

> **I'm in love with the potential of miracles. For me, the safest place is out on a limb.**
>
> *Shirley MacLaine*

“I wanted to be a set
designer when I
was young.”

Judi Dench

> "I think a playwright must be his own dramaturg."
>
> *John Guare*

> Only a man who has felt ultimate despair is capable of feeling ultimate bliss.

Alexandre Dumas

> **The road to success is always under construction.**
>
> *Lily Tomlin*

"People say I make strange choices, but they're not strange for me. My sickness is that I'm fascinated by human behavior, by what's underneath the surface, by the worlds inside people."

Johnny Depp

"I always have something big enough to say as a playwright. It's storytelling.**"**

Tanya Saracho

> "Every action we take, everything we do, is either a victory or defeat in the struggle to become what we want to be."

Anne Bronte

"If a playwright tried to see eye to eye with everybody, he would get the worst case of strabismus since Hannibal lost an eye trying to count his nineteen elephants during a snowstorm while crossing the Alps.

James Thurber

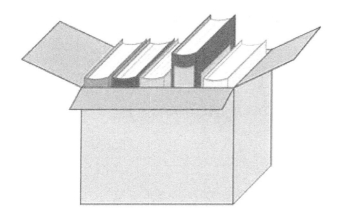

Terminology

Use proper terminology when writing your 'blocking'. If you have your actor moving on a line (which you, for certain, will, use the correct terminology when you do it. Example:

(Crosses left to chair.)

(Waves him down stage.)

(Crosses down.)

(Crosses left.)

(Saunters upstage.)

(Enters.)

(Exits.)

Cast

The list of characters in a play and the actors who play them.

Cheat

To make an action on stage look realistic without actually doing what you seem to be doing; e.g. an actor looking towards the audience in the general direction of the person he is talking to, is cheating.

Beat

A pause in the lines being delivered or a moment before an actor moves/crosses.

Cue

Also used in the sense of the point at which an actor must enter or speak.

Director

In control of all aspects of the production. He/she develops the concept of the production, briefs the designer and lighting designer, plots the actor's moves, rehearses the actors, etc. etc.

Doubling

One actor taking more than one part in a play.

Downstage

Towards the audience.

Upstage

At the back of the stage; away from the audience. As a verb: when one actor deliberately draw the attention of the audience to himself for purely selfish purposes.

Flat

An oblong frame of timber, covered with either canvas or hardboard and painted, which forms part of the set. There are also door flats, window flates, even fireplace flats. Canvas flats, being lighter and easier to move around.

Left

Stage left, or the LHS as you face the audience.

Right

Stage right, or the LHS as you face the audience.

Exit

Actor leaves the stage, exit right or left.

Rake

Many stage floors, usually in theatres built for dance or variety, are higher at the back than at the front, to give the audience a better view. These stages are said to be "raked", and the "rake" is the angle of slope from back to front.

Set Dressing

Items on a set which are not actually used by anyone but which make it look more realistic (e.g. curtains over a window, a bowl of flowers on a table, and so on).

For a complete glossary of theatre terms go to:

https://www.iar.unicamp.br/lab/luz/ld/C%EAnica/Gloss%E1rios/a_glossary_of_teatre_terms.pdf

My favourite story from classic theatre:

Sarah Bernhardt and Gloria Swanson were famous divas of the theatre in the early years of the last century. They were arch enemies and were cast in the same play.

On opening night they had a scene together and as Sarah delivered her lines she took a couple of steps upstage, causing the Gloria to be upstaged. (Making her turn her back to the audience.) Gloria quickly caught on and when she delivered her next lines to Sarah she took several steps upstage.

This went on until they reached the back flats upstage. Sarah Bernhardt then delivered her famous line (under her breath so the audience didn't hear.) "DO YOU CLIMB, DAH-LING?"

"*Being a playwright of any race is difficult, and Lord knows it gets more difficult the further you get from the middle of the road. I don't know what kind of magic my mojo is working, but it's working.*"

Suzan-Lori Parks

Also by
TRISHA SUGAREK

Toe Tag #47
The Ash Can
The Waltz
The Bullies
Curiosity Killed the Cat
A Hint of Magnolia
Love Never Leaves Bruises
Great Expectations
The Perfume Bottle
Straight Edged Secret
Orange Socks
You're Not the Boss of Me!
The 'D' Word
Mean Girls
Training the Troops
Daughterland
The Bard of the Yukon
You're Fat, You're Ugly and You Dress Weird
Cyber-Hate
Forever Yours
The Last Text
If We Break Up, I'll Die!
Mr. Churchill's Cat
A Dime Bag of Weed
The Art of Murder
The Run-Away
Trans-G Kid
The Wedding Crasher
Trans-G Parents
No Means NO!
Black vs. White vs. Brown
Drop the Phone
Parkland Requiem

...more by Trisha Sugarek

Fiction
Women Outside the Walls
Wild Violets
Song of the Yukon
Sisters

True Crime/Mystery Series * World of Murder
Art of Murder
Dance of Murder
Act of Murder
Angel of Murder
Taste of Murder
(Beneath) The Bridge of Murder
Video of Murder

Children's Fiction
Stanley the Stalwart Dragon
The Exciting Exploits of an Effervescent Elf
Bertie, the Bookworm and the Bully Boys
Emma and the Lost Unicorn

Poetry
Butterflies and Bullets
The World of Haiku" with Sumi-E Artwork
Haiku Journal" -- a companion book
Moths and Machetes

To learn more about the author and her books, visit
www.writeratplay.com

Made in the USA
Las Vegas, NV
28 October 2021

33252474R00149